Through a Child's Voice:

Transformational Journaling™

Through a Child's Voice: Transformational Journaling™

Wingfield House of Peace Publications
Pueblo West, CO
Copyright © 2011 Debra A. Wingfield, Ed.D.
ISBN: 978-0-578-08818-1

Disclaimer: This book is a method of journaling. It is not intended to take the place of mental health therapy. Please contact your local mental health professional for psychotherapy.

Note: *The painting on the cover of this book is dedicated to the memory of Brian Klemmer, one of my mentors, who helped me find my voice.*
© 2010 by Debra Wingfield

How to Contact the Author

Debra A. Wingfield, Ed.D.

Wingfield House of Peace Publications

621 N. Blaine Way

Pueblo West, CO

Phone: 719.647.0652

DrDebra@houseofpeacepubs.com

Blog: http://todayskidstomorrowsleaders.com

This book is dedicated to all

the Courageous Kids

who are still in abusive homes

or have returned to their Protective Parent.

Your stories are valuable lessons

about a system that failed you

when your voice was silenced.

http://TodaysKidsTomorrowsLeaders.com

This book is the story of

_____

Dear Parent,

This book is a guide to help you help your children write their childhood story about living with an abuser. This Journal/Workbook is for children removed from the caring and protection of their protective parent and placed in the care and primary parenting of their abusive parent. This journal allows children to write their story as a record of their journey to document what occurs in their lives after parental separation/divorce. The "Focus Points™" for the journal came from the themes of stories written by children at http://CourageousKids.net.

My humble thanks go to the children who shared their stories, their pain, and their triumphs. You are truly precious children who never deserved the abuse and mistreatment at the hands of your parent and the Family Courts. Your stories are a shining light to children still caught in the trap of living with an abusive parent. There is an end to your suffering and a time for healing to create a life of happiness and peace.

How to help your children use this Journal

Make this journal a special book for your child. Write their name in it when you give it to them. Explain what they share on the following pages is their voice. They are free to keep it very private, share it with you or other trusted adults, or use it to make a public declaration through http://CourageousKids.net.

There is room to write their story, draw their feelings, or use in any way they find expresses their experience.

For younger children, they may need some help from you to understand the "Focus Points™". A word about what "Focus Points™" are. "Focus Points™" are designed to help the writer focus their thoughts and feelings by giving a starting point to begin writing. When my daughter was young, we used to create stories by one of us starting a sentence and the other one completing it. This is also a good way to give your children an example of how they can

 ©2011 House of Peace Publications All Rights Reserved
http://TodaysKidsTomorrowsLeaders.com

work with their journal "Focus Points™". Make your example fun and interesting for your child. For example, you could say, "one day a Mommy and her little girl went..." Then, the child would finish with "to the park to play on the swings. The little girl liked to..." Then, the mommy would finish with "swing as high as possible and try to touch the sky. The little girl would ask her mommy to ..." I know you have the idea now.

In healing and living a peace-filled and joyful life,

Dr. Debra

P.S. A portion of the sales of this book are donated to Protective Parents organizations.

Dear Courageous Child,

This book is for you to tell what happened in your life. Write about your life before your parents separated. Write about your life after your parents separated. Everyone has a different story about their life. You may even find your story different from your brothers and sisters. There is no right or wrong way to go through your life. It is just how it is for you, and no one else.

This book is just for you to put together in your own way. You may want to share it with a trusted adult. You may even choose to share this book with other courageous kids. Your life may include hearing your parent being told what to do by your other parent. Your life may be about seeing your parent hurt or injured by your other parent. Your life may be about being abused. There are many different types of abuse and control used by parents toward each other or towards you.

Here are some types of abuse and/or control you may have heard or seen.

- Intimidation tactics-- this is where one parent may try to make another parent do things with angry looks; movements of their hands or body or both; or with hurtful words.

- Isolation tactics-- this is where one parent may try to keep the other parent away from family or friends; going to work; leaving the house alone; or speaking to anyone on the phone.

- Economic/Financial tactics-- this is where one parent may try to stop the other parent from getting or keeping a job; not give them money or blame them for spending money on things that are not needed; or use other behaviors to keep a parent from having money. They may blame the other parent for spending money on food; rent or house payments; or necessary clothes when they want to spend money on drinking, drugging, or gambling.

- Threats-- this is where one parent may use threats or threatening behavior toward the other parent. These may be statements that they will injure or harm the other parent if they don't do what they are told to do. Threats can also be breaking things or punching holes in walls or doors. The goal of threats is to let the other parent know that the next time they may actually hit them.

- Using Children-- this is where one parent may say they will take the children away from the other parent; keep the children from the other parent by going to court to get custody of them; or telling the other parent if they leave, they will take the children away from them or report them to social services. One parent may ask the children to spy on the other parent, then report back anything the other parent does during the day.

- Emotional Abuse-- this is where one parent may use words to hurt the other parent by calling them names; or giving long lectures about what the parent is doing wrong; or how they should do something even if they don't do it themselves. One parent may stop talking to the other parent for several hours or several days or weeks at a time. One parent may twist the words of the other parent around to make it look like they are the bad parent and the good parent is the one who is abusive.

- Using Male Privilege-- this is where the father may use superiority over the mother and claim they know what is best for her and everyone else in the family. He may demand meals be prepared in a certain way. He may demand the house be cleaned a certain way. He may expect everyone in the house to take care of him even when other family members have problems.

- Minimizing, Denying, Blaming-- this is where one parent may say what they did to hurt the other parent or the children wasn't that bad; or it wasn't their fault; or make the other parent responsible for what happened even if the other parent was not involved.

- Control tactics-- this is where one parent may use words, actions, or behaviors to force the other parent to do what they want them to do; when they want them to do it; and how they want them to do it.

- Spiritual abuse-- this is where one parent may only allow the other parent to go to church if they say it is okay; make them practice their religion even if that is not the other parent's belief; or make fun of any spiritual or religious groups or beliefs that the other parent has.

- Non-physical sexual abuse-- this is where one parent may say things about the other parent's looks, clothes, or call them bad names related to their gender. They may accuse the other parent of having affairs or sexual relationships when they are out of the house.

- Physical and physical sexual abuse-- this is where one parent may use physical violence to control the other parent by hitting, scratching, choking, slapping, spitting at the other parent; or any other physical contact with the other parent that causes injury, pain or bruising. One parent may force another parent to be touched in their private areas in front of the children, or to leave the children unattended while they go to the bedroom to have sex.

Each page in this book gives you a place to write, draw, or tell about your life. Each page starts with a sentence starter ("Focus Point™") to help you start your writing, drawing, or original response. Some of the pages may not fit for your life. You can skip over them or come back to them later if something changes that brings up the area identified by the sentence starter ("Focus Point™").

The most important thing to remember is *this is your life story*. No one else has exactly the same life story as you. If you want to read about other "Courageous Kids" who wrote their life stories, go to http://CourageousKids.net. Their stories helped me come up with the sentence starters ("Focus Points™") for your book.

If you ever have any questions about the sentence starters ("Focus Points™"), or what you are going through, feel free to contact me at http://TodaysKidsTomorrowsLeaders.com/

Remember, no child or adult ever should be hurt or abused by another person.

Peacefully yours,

Dr. Debra

http://TodaysKidsTomorrowsLeaders.com   11

Beginnings

Start your journal with two facts:

I was _____ years old when my parents separated.

I am _____ years old now.

What I remember about the day my parents separated is_____

_____

_____

_____

_____

_____

_____

_____

_____

_____

_____

_____

_____

http://TodaysKidsTomorrowsLeaders.com

_____

_____

_____

_____

_____

_____

_____

_____

_____

_____

_____

_____

_____

_____

_____

_____

_____

_____

_____

_____

_____

The parent who took care of me most before the separation was

_____

_____

_____

_____

_____

_____

_____

_____

_____

_____

_____

_____

_____

_____

_____

_____

http://TodaysKidsTomorrowsLeaders.com

_____

_____

_____

_____

_____

_____

_____

_____

_____

_____

_____

_____

_____

_____

_____

_____

The parent who attended school conferences, activities, and other events with me or made sure I attended these events before the separation was _____

_____

_____

_____

_____

_____

_____

_____

_____

_____

_____

_____

_____

_____

_____

http://TodaysKidsTomorrowsLeaders.com

_____

_____

_____

_____

_____

_____

_____

_____

_____

_____

_____

_____

_____

_____

_____

_____

_____

The parent who took me to the doctor before the separation

was _____

_____

_____

_____

_____

_____

_____

_____

_____

_____

_____

_____

_____

_____

_____

_____

_____

_____

_____

_____

_____

_____

_____

_____

_____

_____

_____

_____

_____

_____

_____

_____

_____

_____

_____

_____

_____

The parent who left work to take care of me if I was sick or

injured before the separation was _____

_____

_____

_____

_____

_____

_____

_____

_____

_____

_____

_____

_____

_____

_____

_____

http://TodaysKidsTomorrowsLeaders.com

The parenting battle went on for _____ years; It is still going

on or ended in _____ year. The state/country where I was

living during the parenting battle is _____

_____

_____

_____

_____

_____

_____

_____

_____

_____

_____

_____

_____

_____

_____

_____

_____

_____

_____

_____

_____

_____

_____

_____

_____

_____

_____

_____

_____

_____

_____

_____

_____

_____

_____

The primary parent I wanted to be with is _____

because_____

_____

_____

_____

_____

_____

_____

_____

_____

_____

_____

_____

_____

_____

_____

_____

_____

http://TodaysKidsTomorrowsLeaders.com

_____

_____

_____

_____

_____

_____

_____

_____

_____

_____

_____

_____

_____

_____

_____

_____

_____

_____

The parent I did not want to live with is _____ because

_____

_____

_____

_____

_____

_____

_____

_____

_____

_____

_____

_____

_____

_____

_____

http://TodaysKidsTomorrowsLeaders.com

_____

_____

_____

_____

_____

_____

_____

_____

_____

_____

_____

_____

_____

_____

_____

_____

_____

_____

It would be _____ to live with the

parent I did not want to be with because _____

_____

_____

_____

_____

_____

_____

_____

_____

_____

_____

_____

_____

_____

_____

_____

_____

_____

_____

_____

_____

_____

_____

_____

_____

_____

_____

_____

_____

_____

_____

_____

_____

_____

_____

The court listened to my wishes to live with my _____.The court did not listen to my wishes to live with my _____.

What I understand about the court's decision about which parent the court chose for me to live with is _____

_____

_____

_____

_____

_____

_____

_____

_____

_____

_____

_____

_____

_____

http://TodaysKidsTomorrowsLeaders.com

_____

_____

_____

_____

_____

_____

_____

_____

_____

_____

_____

_____

_____

_____

_____

_____

_____

My experience with the adults brought into help my parents

with the divorce was_____

_____

_____

_____

_____

_____

_____

_____

_____

_____

_____

_____

_____

_____

_____

The results in my life of the adults involved in my parent's divorce that were supposed to protect me/help me was __

_____

_____

_____

_____

_____

_____

_____

_____

_____

_____

_____

_____

_____

_____

_____

_____

_____

_____

_____

_____

_____

_____

_____

_____

_____

_____

_____

_____

_____

_____

_____

_____

_____

_____

_____

My experience with the adults who were there to help me when
they listened and worked with my mother during her divorce
was _____

_____

_____

_____

_____

_____

_____

_____

_____

_____

_____

_____

_____

_____

_____

_____

_____

_____

_____

_____

_____

_____

_____

_____

_____

_____

_____

_____

_____

_____

_____

_____

_____

The ability for my mother to get court involved adults to

understand what happened before the separation was ____

_____

_____

_____

_____

_____

_____

_____

_____

_____

_____

_____

_____

_____

_____

http://TodaysKidsTomorrowsLeaders.com

_____

_____

_____

_____

_____

_____

_____

_____

_____

_____

_____

_____

_____

_____

_____

_____

My experience with the adults who were there to help me when

they listened and worked with my father during his divorce was

_____

_____

_____

_____

_____

_____

_____

_____

_____

_____

_____

_____

_____

_____

_____

The ability for my father to get court involved adults to

understand what happened before the separation was____

_____

_____

_____

_____

_____

_____

_____

_____

_____

_____

_____

_____

_____

_____

_____

_____

I found the adults who I talked to about what I wanted to

happen about time spent with my mother was_____

_____

_____

_____

_____

_____

_____

_____

_____

_____

_____

_____

_____

_____

_____

_____

_____

_____

_____

_____

_____

_____

_____

_____

_____

_____

_____

_____

_____

_____

_____

_____

_____

_____

_____

I found the adults who I talked to about what I wanted to

happen about time spent with my father was_____

_____

_____

_____

_____

_____

_____

_____

_____

_____

_____

_____

_____

_____

_____

_____

_____

_____

_____

_____

_____

_____

_____

_____

_____

_____

_____

_____

_____

_____

_____

_____

_____

_____

_____

I was/was not allowed to talk to the judge about the time I

wanted to be with my parent's because _____

_____

_____

_____

_____

_____

_____

_____

_____

_____

_____

_____

_____

_____

_____

http://TodaysKidsTomorrowsLeaders.com

_____

_____

_____

_____

_____

_____

_____

_____

_____

_____

_____

_____

_____

_____

_____

_____

I saw my mother/father have money problems through the

divorce and afterwards because _____

_____

_____

_____

_____

_____

_____

_____

_____

_____

_____

_____

_____

_____

_____

http://TodaysKidsTomorrowsLeaders.com

Therapy/counseling happened during/after the divorce because

_____

_____

_____

_____

_____

_____

_____

_____

_____

_____

_____

_____

_____

_____

_____

_____

What I learned from therapy was _____

_____

_____

_____

_____

_____

_____

_____

_____

_____

_____

_____

_____

_____

_____

_____

_____

_____

http://TodaysKidsTomorrowsLeaders.com

I was/was not allowed to object to what adults said who were

supposed to protect/help me either directly or through my

court-appointed attorney because _____

_____

_____

_____

_____

_____

_____

_____

_____

_____

_____

_____

_____

_____

_____

http://TodaysKidsTomorrowsLeaders.com

My brothers, sisters, or I was physically abused by a parent

before/after the separation by _____

_____

_____

_____

_____

_____

_____

_____

_____

_____

_____

_____

_____

_____

_____

_____

_____

http://TodaysKidsTomorrowsLeaders.com

My brothers, sisters, or I was emotionally abused by a parent

before/after the separation by_____

_____

_____

_____

_____

_____

_____

_____

_____

_____

_____

_____

_____

_____

_____

_____

http://TodaysKidsTomorrowsLeaders.com

_____

_____

_____

_____

_____

_____

_____

_____

_____

_____

_____

_____

_____

_____

_____

_____

My brothers, sisters, or I was sexually abused by a parent

before/after the separation by_____

_____

_____

_____

_____

_____

_____

_____

_____

_____

_____

_____

_____

_____

_____

_____

http://TodaysKidsTomorrowsLeaders.com

_____

_____

_____

_____

_____

_____

_____

_____

_____

_____

_____

_____

_____

_____

_____

_____

_____

_____

_____

_____

_____

My brothers, sisters, or I was neglected by a parent before/after

the separation by _____

_____

_____

_____

_____

_____

_____

_____

_____

_____

_____

_____

_____

_____

_____

_____

_____

_____

_____

_____

_____

_____

_____

_____

_____

_____

_____

_____

_____

_____

_____

_____

_____

I made reports of child abuse to police or social services/child

protective services because _____

_____

_____

_____

_____

_____

_____

_____

_____

_____

_____

_____

_____

_____

_____

_____

http://TodaysKidsTomorrowsLeaders.com

_____

_____

_____

_____

_____

_____

_____

_____

_____

_____

_____

_____

_____

_____

_____

_____

_____

The adults I reported child abuse to did or said _____

_____

_____

_____

_____

_____

_____

_____

_____

_____

_____

_____

_____

_____

_____

_____

http://TodaysKidsTomorrowsLeaders.com

_____

_____

_____

_____

_____

_____

_____

_____

_____

_____

_____

_____

_____

_____

_____

_____

_____

Other adults outside my family made reports of child abuse to

police or social services because _____

_____

_____

_____

_____

_____

_____

_____

_____

_____

_____

_____

_____

_____

_____

_____

_____

_____

_____

_____

_____

_____

_____

_____

_____

_____

_____

_____

_____

_____

_____

_____

_____

_____

_____

The ways the abuse changed my whole life (school, friends,

other family members) is_____

_____

_____

_____

_____

_____

_____

_____

_____

_____

_____

_____

_____

_____

_____

http://TodaysKidsTomorrowsLeaders.com

One of my parents was dishonest about child abuse by the

other parent when they_____

_____

_____

_____

_____

_____

_____

_____

_____

_____

_____

_____

_____

_____

_____

_____

http://TodaysKidsTomorrowsLeaders.com

One of my parents was dishonest about drug abuse or mental

illness by the other parent by_____

_____

_____

_____

_____

_____

_____

_____

_____

_____

_____

_____

_____

_____

_____

_____

_____

_____

_____

_____

_____

_____

_____

_____

_____

_____

_____

_____

_____

_____

_____

_____

_____

_____

_____

_____

One of my parents got in the way of or stopped my other

parent from working by _____

_____

_____

_____

_____

_____

_____

_____

_____

_____

_____

_____

_____

_____

_____

_____

_____

http://TodaysKidsTomorrowsLeaders.com

_____

_____

_____

_____

_____

_____

_____

_____

_____

_____

_____

_____

_____

_____

_____

_____

_____

_____

_____

One of my parents remarried and what happened was ___

_____

_____

_____

_____

_____

_____

_____

_____

_____

_____

_____

_____

_____

_____

_____

_____

_____

_____

_____

_____

_____

_____

_____

_____

_____

_____

_____

_____

_____

_____

_____

I was lied to by a parent to make me do what they wanted me to

do by telling me _____

_____

_____

_____

_____

_____

_____

_____

_____

_____

_____

_____

_____

_____

_____

_____

_____

_____

http://TodaysKidsTomorrowsLeaders.com

One of my parents was blamed for trying to keep me away from

my other parent by _____

_____

_____

_____

_____

_____

_____

_____

_____

_____

_____

_____

_____

_____

_____

_____

_____

http://TodaysKidsTomorrowsLeaders.com

_____

_____

_____

_____

_____

_____

_____

_____

_____

_____

_____

_____

_____

_____

_____

_____

_____

_____

I was taken by one of my parents and forced to live with my

other parent because_____

_____

_____

_____

_____

_____

_____

_____

_____

_____

_____

_____

_____

_____

_____

_____

http://TodaysKidsTomorrowsLeaders.com

_____

_____

_____

_____

_____

_____

_____

_____

_____

_____

_____

_____

_____

_____

_____

_____

_____

_____

_____

I felt forced by someone to take me to my other parent because

_____

_____

_____

_____

_____

_____

_____

_____

_____

_____

_____

_____

_____

_____

_____

_____

I was locked up in a juvenile facility or psychiatric hospital to

stop me from telling the truth about being abused because

_____

_____

_____

_____

_____

_____

_____

_____

_____

_____

_____

_____

_____

_____

_____

_____

_____

_____

_____

_____

_____

_____

_____

_____

_____

_____

_____

_____

_____

_____

_____

_____

I finally got away from my abusive parent by _____

_____

_____

_____

_____

_____

_____

_____

_____

_____

_____

_____

_____

_____

_____

_____

The adult who listened to my story and helped me was___

_____

_____

_____

_____

_____

_____

_____

_____

_____

_____

_____

_____

_____

_____

_____

One of my parents said they would commit suicide one or more

times because _____

_____

_____

_____

_____

_____

_____

_____

_____

_____

_____

_____

_____

_____

_____

_____

_____

_____

_____

_____

_____

_____

_____

_____

_____

_____

_____

_____

_____

_____

_____

_____

One of my parents said they would kill me or my other parent if

_____

_____

_____

_____

_____

_____

_____

_____

_____

_____

_____

_____

_____

_____

_____

_____

_____

_____

_____

_____

_____

_____

_____

_____

_____

_____

_____

_____

_____

_____

_____

_____

One parent threatened/said they would commit suicide or kill family members before/after my parents separated if ____

_____

_____

_____

_____

_____

_____

_____

_____

_____

_____

_____

_____

_____

_____

_____

During the separation or after the parenting plan was made, my primary parent stopped me from seeing or speaking to my other parent by_____

_____

_____

_____

_____

_____

_____

_____

_____

_____

_____

_____

_____

_____

http://TodaysKidsTomorrowsLeaders.com

I was able to go back to live with my protective parent after

_____

_____

_____

_____

_____

_____

_____

_____

_____

_____

_____

_____

_____

_____

_____

_____

_____

_____

_____

_____

_____

_____

_____

_____

_____

_____

_____

_____

_____

_____

_____

_____

Primary parenting was/was not transferred to this parent

because_____

_____

_____

_____

_____

_____

_____

_____

_____

_____

_____

_____

_____

_____

_____

_____

_____

_____

_____

_____

_____

_____

_____

_____

_____

_____

_____

_____

_____

_____

_____

_____

_____

_____

_____

_____

I was able to go back to live with my protective parent, but my

abusive parent did things to get back at me for leaving by

_____

_____

_____

_____

_____

_____

_____

_____

_____

_____

_____

_____

_____

_____

_____

_____

_____

_____

_____

_____

_____

_____

_____

_____

_____

_____

_____

_____

_____

_____

_____

_____

_____

_____

_____

_____

_____

_____

I ran away from my abusive parent because _____

_____

_____

_____

_____

_____

_____

_____

_____

_____

_____

_____

_____

_____

_____

_____

_____

_____

http://TodaysKidsTomorrowsLeaders.com

_____

_____

_____

_____

_____

_____

_____

_____

_____

_____

_____

_____

_____

_____

_____

_____

_____

I was _____ years old. I was in runaway status for _

___ years. I was helped by _____

_____

_____

_____

_____

_____

_____

_____

_____

_____

_____

_____

_____

_____

_____

_____

http://TodaysKidsTomorrowsLeaders.com

_____

_____

_____

_____

_____

_____

_____

_____

_____

_____

_____

_____

_____

_____

_____

_____

_____

One of my parents was put in jail or on probation because of

something the other parent did or said about them because

_____

_____

_____

_____

_____

_____

_____

_____

_____

_____

_____

_____

_____

_____

_____

_____

_____

_____

_____

_____

_____

_____

_____

_____

_____

_____

_____

_____

_____

_____

_____

_____

_____

The charges were untrue because_____

_____

_____

_____

_____

_____

_____

_____

_____

_____

_____

_____

_____

_____

_____

_____

_____

http://TodaysKidsTomorrowsLeaders.com

The parent who was jailed was _____

_____

_____

_____

_____

_____

_____

_____

_____

_____

_____

_____

_____

_____

_____

_____

_____

_____

_____

_____

_____

_____

_____

_____

_____

_____

_____

_____

_____

_____

_____

_____

_____

_____

_____

_____

What I would like to have happened differently in my case is

_____

_____

_____

_____

_____

_____

_____

_____

_____

_____

_____

_____

_____

_____

_____

_____

http://TodaysKidsTomorrowsLeaders.com

_____

_____

_____

_____

_____

_____

_____

_____

_____

_____

_____

_____

_____

_____

_____

_____

_____

_____

_____

The way I feel about my life since my parents separated is

_____

_____

_____

_____

_____

_____

_____

_____

_____

_____

_____

_____

_____

_____

_____

_____

What I want to add to my story is _____

_____

_____

_____

_____

_____

_____

_____

_____

_____

_____

_____

_____

_____

_____

_____

How I want to live my life from today forward is_____

_____

_____

_____

_____

_____

_____

_____

_____

_____

_____

_____

_____

_____

_____

_____

_____

_____

http://TodaysKidsTomorrowsLeaders.com

_____

_____

_____

_____

_____

_____

_____

_____

_____

_____

_____

_____

_____

_____

_____

_____

_____

_____

_____

The type of relationship partner I want to be is_____

_____

_____

_____

_____

_____

_____

_____

_____

_____

_____

_____

_____

_____

_____

_____

_____

_____

_____

_____

_____

_____

_____

_____

_____

_____

_____

_____

_____

_____

_____

_____

_____

_____

http://TodaysKidsTomorrowsLeaders.com

The type of relationship partner I want to have is_____

_____

_____

_____

_____

_____

_____

_____

_____

_____

_____

_____

_____

_____

_____

_____

_____

_____

_____

_____

_____

_____

_____

_____

_____

_____

_____

_____

_____

_____

_____

_____

_____

_____

_____

How I want to handle relationship conflicts is_____

_____

_____

_____

_____

_____

_____

_____

_____

_____

_____

_____

_____

_____

_____

_____

_____

How I want to share emotions in relationships is_____

_____

_____

_____

_____

_____

_____

_____

_____

_____

_____

_____

_____

_____

_____

_____

_____

_____

_____

_____

_____

_____

_____

_____

_____

_____

_____

_____

_____

_____

_____

_____

The type of home atmosphere I want to have is_____

_____

_____

_____

_____

_____

_____

_____

_____

_____

_____

_____

_____

_____

_____

_____

http://TodaysKidsTomorrowsLeaders.com

www.ingramcontent.com/pod-product-compliance
Lightning Source LLC
Chambersburg PA
CBHW031515040426
42445CB00009B/236